TITLE PAGE

THE OATMAN ARIZONA HOLY LAND TOUR
The Bible Chiseled In Stone

© by James Russell, January 2004, ©February 2006. All rights reserved. No part of this publication may be reproduced in any form or by any means without prior written permission of the author or publisher.

"The Oatman Arizona Holy Land Tour"
Printed in the United States of America
Published by James Russell / SAN 295-852X

"The Oatman Arizona Holy Land Tour"
Written by James Russell © January 2004, ©February 2006
Illustrations / Photos by James Russell
ISBN-10 No. 0-916367- 17 – 7 First Printed Edition©February 2006
ISBN-13: No. 978-0-916367-17-6 same edition as above.

Categories: History, Biblical, Old West Arizona, Route 66 Auto Tour, Motorcycle Tour Guide. BISAC Subject Heading: RELO70000 Religion/ Christianity. TRV025120 Travel/United States/West/Arizona

Legal Notice::
Author, publisher and seller assume no liabilities whatsoever. Sold as information only. Adult supervision required for minors when taking the Oatman Arizona Holy Land Tour.

To Contact Author:
Type into any Internet search engine the words; "James Russell Publishing." This will bring you to the Web site where you can find our address, e-mail, etc. http://www.JamesRussellPublishing.com

This book can be purchased from:
Any bookstore can order this book. Give them the ISBN numbers listed above.

DEDICATED TO:

The Following Bible Quotes

....

DEDICATED TO:
Yahweh, Yeshua, Jesus of Nazareth - King of Kings, Lord of Lords.

....

INSURANCE POLICY
"Blessed is he that considereth the poor: the Lord will deliver him in time of trouble."

....

PROMISES
The King James Version Bible has well over 800 promises. Have you read them?

....

TABLE OF CONTENTS

TITLE PAGE 1

DEDICATED TO: 2

PREFACE 6

SPECIAL THANKS 6

A NEW TOURIST ATTRACTION 6

   MEDIA FAIR USE 6

   PROOF OF DISCOVERY 6

A CHRISTIAN BOOK 7

HOLY LAND REINACTMENTS 7

BOOK VERSION PHOTO QUALITY 8

E-BOOK VERSION 8

INSTRUCTIONS 9

HOW TO USE THIS BOOK 9

RESETTING ODOMETER 9

DRIVER INSTRUCTION – DANGER! 9

Table of Contents

HOW WILL YOU BENEFIT? 10

CHRISTIAN SCHOOL 10

AUTHOR'S REQUEST 11

IMPROVEMENTS NEEDED 11

LARGELY UNDISCOVERED 12

CAUTION 12

OATMAN, ARIZONA 12

BIBLICAL DONKEY FACTS 13

HISTORICAL INTEREST 13

HOW THE HOLY LAND TOUR BEGAN 14

THE AUTHOR 16

THE MANY NAMES OF THE LORD 17

CHAPTER 1 18

BEGIN TOUR #1 18

CHAPTER 2 31

Table of Contents

BEGIN TOUR #2 31

CHAPTER 3 40

BEGIN TOUR #3 40

CHAPTER 4 76

BEGIN TOUR #4 76

THE THRONE ROOM OF GOD 82

END OF THE TOUR 89

TO LEARN MORE 89

EXTRA OATMAN PAGES 90

PERSONAL NOTES PAGE 93

PERSONAL NOTES PAGE 94

BOOK CATALOG 95

PREFACE
SPECIAL THANKS

To the Lord Jesus of Nazareth. I thank the Lord for opening my eyes to see what was hidden and to present this tour book to honor God and His Word to benefit all who come here. May your salvation and your miracle begin!

A NEW TOURIST ATTRACTION

The Oatman, Arizona Holy Land Tour is seventeen miles south of Laughlin, Nevada and is a new tourist attraction due to the numerous natural Biblical land formations (rock art) chiseled in stone. The local resident and tourist will be enlightened and entertained with the sheer natural beauty of the self-guided tour with a Biblical theme.

MEDIA FAIR USE

This book is copyrighted. Writers and media can quote from the book to produce articles and news stories as long as the article or story does not exceed 30% quotations. If you require more quotes, please contact the author and publisher for written permission. In all cases, you must mention in your story for readers or television viewers to visit "James RussellPublishing.com" Web site. If you develop a sales brochure or flyer based on this book and the Oatman Arizona Holy Land Tour to promote your town, special event or business please do mention in your brochure for readers to visit the "JamesRussellPublishing.com" Web site. Since James Russell discovered The Oatman Arizona Holy Land Tour please give him full credit and, by sending people to our Web site. If you need to or use any of our photos we also ask the same courtesy for credits. Exceeding these general terms or omitting credits can result in a copyright violation. If you wish to include this book as a prize in advertising or promotional contests you may do so! Thank you.

PROOF OF DISCOVERY

For hundreds of years there is no record of any Biblical related scenes in the Oatman, Arizona area. The Indians, missionaries, miners, wagon train emigrants, motorized vehicles using Route 66, movie studios came and went and still no record was made. Even today in the tourist era there were no brochures, articles or even hearsay indicating there was anything Biblical in the mountains and valleys nearby. Only when the writing of this book occurred did so many Biblical rock formations become known to the public. The author and discoverer James Russell states,

"If the Lord God did not open my eyes I too never would have seen or found any of these rock formations. All credit to the Lord for He opened my eyes and enabled me to write this book. This is the Lord's doing."

A CHRISTIAN BOOK

This is not a Catholic book. It is not a Southern Baptist, Jehovah Witness, a Mormon book or any other denominational book. It is a Christian book of no specific denomination. Therefore, no denomination may claim authority over the Bible scenes herein. It is a book based on the Holy Bible (King James Version) and is simply a Christian tour book based on the written word in the Bible.

Any church or denomination that attempts to claim authority or ownership rights to the Bible scene locations is invalid. It all belongs to God! The Oatman Arizona Holy Land Tour is not a substitute for the authentic Holy Land in Israel, but we do have some similarities here worth visiting. After seeing The Oatman Arizona Holy Land Tour you may want to see the real thing in Israel.

HOLY LAND REINACTMENTS

This would be an ideal place to conduct Biblical reenactments and live Holy Land theme theatrical play productions. Here in Oatman, Arizona is the place it should be done. Roman citizens, Egyptians, Pharisees, zealots and soldiers could walk about the sites, chariot races and even actors dressed as angels, slaves, Moses, Jesus, Caesar, Pharaoh and prophets could preach nearby. Like the Renaissance Fair with a Biblical theme, miracles and gladiator battle reenactments could be performed and even Jesus' last days and resurrection portrayed. Mid-March would be a good month as the Snowbirds are still present and the weather is generally mild. It will be a Holy Land experience in a natural outdoor setting. This could be a seven-day annual springtime fair (with special events for Christmas and Easter). The local churches and college theatrical departments could easily launch this event with the talent pool they already have. It will also be a great witnessing tool so people can experience the Bible first hand as if being there themselves in the days Christ walked the earth. Perhaps an authentic Holy Land themed village will one day be constructed nearby to shop and dine with the Romans, the Jews and the Christians. Authentic era tent markets could be erected all along south Rt. 66 from Moses Rock to Topock for special events. It would be fun. We will need some camels but Oatman already has the horses and donkeys, just like it was in the Holy Land!

BOOK VERSION PHOTO QUALITY

The resolution of the photos in the e-book version must be low so they can be downloaded electronically. The print version will have larger photo files depending on the quality of the photos and may or may not meet professional photography expectations. Author and publisher are not offering a warrantee of photographic quality in any version of the book. The print version of the book may or may not have black & white photographs.

E-BOOK VERSION

The e-book version will permit the purchaser to print one copy of the book to paper format. We do not authorize any copies of the printed version of the book. It is the purchaser's responsibility to ensure printer is serviced with full ink cartridges and paper tray is full and printer is turned on before printing the file. You may only get one try to print the book so make sure your computer and printer are up to the task. There are about 70 full-color photos in the e-book, so install new ink black and color cartridges and test them to make sure they work before printing the book.

Preface

INSTRUCTIONS

Odometer miles varies from vehicle to vehicle. The miles indicated may be off a tenth or two here or there, so just make a mental adjustment if the miles do not match exactly. If you miss a site you can likely see it at the next stop. If not, just turn around later and come back to it, but do so in a safe and sane manner. Don't be in a hurry. Relax and enjoy the day.

HOW TO USE THIS BOOK

Bring this book with you with a King James Version Bible (with old and new Testaments), stop to see the point of interest and read the Bible verse (included in the text herein) to experience the full impact of history and to experience the presence of the Lord.

RESETTING ODOMETER

At the beginning of each tour you will be instructed to reset your vehicle trip meter odometer to zero. This is indicated in **dark bold print**. During the tour you will be instructed to, "Go 1.2 miles" to see a site, then you will be asked to "go 2.0 miles" to the next site of interest. To make it easier on yourself, it is wise to simply reset the trip meter odometer to zero at each point of interest. Keep in mind that odometers do vary from vehicle to vehicle, so if you are instructed to go 1.4 miles, your odometer may be off and only read 1.2 miles or perhaps 1.6 miles. You will need to make mile adjustments to correct the error. It may only mean adding or subtracting a tenth of a mile.

DRIVER INSTRUCTION – DANGER!

Whoever does the driving must realize that they may not see all the sites on the first pass through the canyon. You must pay attention to driving. The canyon is narrow and unforgiving of any error. It is easy to tumble off the road into a deep ravine. The driver must remain focused on driving. Stop the vehicle off the road and park when instructed and you should see most all of the sites. Drive slow, let vehicles pass and do not stop in the middle of the road for any reason. Watch out for wild donkeys in the road. Do not approach donkeys out of the town limits. The wild ones will kick and bite. Motorcycles need to be aware of rocks, sand and slippery donkey waste in the road. Bikes do tend to fall down near the Gold Road Gold Mine area due to the awfully tight switchback turns and the rough road surface in the switches. Turn off the loud stereo music. This is a quiet place to be respected. And be Christian courteous even if you are not a Christian (yet).

HOW WILL YOU BENEFIT?

For many, this will be an experience of introduction to God's Word and a chance to learn of the Bible and a few of the many wonderful miracles and promises. For those who already know the Lord and love His Word (the Bible) this will be an awesome experience to uplift your faith. I know the Lord will meet you here. As you call out to Him for deliverance from your affliction He will hear your cry and answer you. Read Psalm 30:2. Believe Him! Dare to believe! Ask for your miracle and seek the Word of God that promises it to you. Just being here visiting the sites is a great step of faith, so come and be with the Lord and spend time with Him. And if you feel like shouting to God for help, go ahead! This is the place! Read Psalm 3:4.

CHRISTIAN SCHOOL

Take the kids (and adults) for a tour and let them use their imagination to find "new" Bible scenes. There are many more the author has left out of this book, so others can make discoveries that will be special to them. This is a fun way to learn the Bible!

- Prayer requests could be attached to creosote bushes, but that can create litter. It is best to place the request on a rock and place a stone on top to pin it down. This way wind will not blow them away.
- Some may want to launch small helium balloons and let the prayer request rise up to heaven. A good launching pad area is at The Lord's Mountain. This place will permit the balloon to rise above the high peaks and actually get to heaven!
- Everyone needs to understand the hazards of the desert creatures, sunburn, dehydration, etc., so responsible adults must be on the scene. Call the Boy and Girl Scouts! Let them patrol the area and give nature walks.
- Decorate a Creosote bush with Christmas ornaments. Use wire, not a hook to attach items or the wind will blow ornaments away.

- Tell others to come take the tour. It is one way to share the Gospel and the mysteries of this wonderful place.

AUTHOR'S REQUEST

Please do not construct or operate shrines or install statues of saints or prophets that intercepts people's direct access to God. Use imagination, not idols. People have a bad habit of praying to statues, relics or worshipping other things except God Himself (whom cannot be seen. Read Matthew 6:6.). This bad habit is described in the Bible and continues today.

It is fine to supply seating areas and nature walks with plaques describing the Biblical scene and also the geology, vegetation, birds and animals that inhabit the area. I request the gold mine owner to preserve the "Gates of Hell" site near Route 66 and all land owners to preserve views and the sites themselves so the public can enjoy them.

One day this Oatman Holy Land Tour will grow in size and may be the only place in the USA with so many distinctive Biblical scenes made not by man's hand all in one location. It is truly unique! Let us not improve upon it in such a way that we offend God, so please operate this Holy Land in a Biblically accurate manner. Let God's commands as stated in the Bible be honored here. It is His creation to be a blessing to us all.

IMPROVEMENTS NEEDED

Parking places are needed, but a shuttle bus or open air tram system to ferry passengers along this thin winding road will work. At each bus stop a walking trail to the site would be nice, but most people are not going to walk far from Rt.66. Maybe another road, like some sections of the old stagecoach road or the utility company road could be used which is much closer to the actual formations, at least on the east side of Sitgreaves Pass. Some restrooms will be needed and benches to rest tired feet. Handicap access would be nice too. All of this takes money, so a percentage of any tour ticket or product sales could help finance improvements and feed the golden goose.

LARGELY UNDISCOVERED

The mountains here are generally accessible by vehicle even in the secluded valleys (this Oatman Holy Land Tour will remain on paved surfaces). Backpackers, rock collectors and nature lovers will find this area attractive when they discover it. So will cliff climbers will love to climb these forbidding walls of rock when they discover this area. The Oatman Holy Land Tour should give the area good exposure as a fine outdoor recreational destination. There are more Biblical rock art formations, but these are left for you to find. Keep your eyes peeled and you may discover more Biblical rock formations!

CAUTION

Please drive slow. Do not stop your vehicle in the road. Use the pull out areas so you will not get hit from behind. Be careful as some pull out areas are narrow and on the edge of a cliff. Do use vehicle pullouts to let other vehicles pass. Never stand in the roadway as cars can come around the blind corners quickly and you may get hit. You can see the sites without standing in the street. Do not drive a large motor home or trailer in this canyon. There are hairpin switchbacks you will get stuck in and you will need to be towed. Nothing over 40 feet long is permitted! You should wear tall leather boots if you plan to walk anywhere on this tour. The plants and stray needles are unforgiving and painful. Do watch out for rattlesnakes, scorpions and large lizards. You will have no problem if you wear boots and walk with a heavy footstep. Kick a rock with your foot before picking it up in your hand. It is not safe to sit down in Arizona unless you are sitting on bare rock. It is easy to twist an ankle in this rough country, so wear boots. Stay clear of rodent holes, wash boots and clothing just in case you were exposed to the Hanta virus. Apply sunscreen and bring water and some salty food with you. Use typical desert protection procedures. Lock your vehicle before hiking anywhere.

OATMAN, ARIZONA

Here is an old western gold mining town where the long gone prospector's donkeys (burros, donkey, ass) still roam the streets and alleys. Busloads of people arrive just to see, pet and feed them. But now there is more to see than just downtown Oatman, much more! The surrounding desert mountains are so diverse it looks like the land Moses and Jesus walked! Before we begin the Oatman Holy Land Tour here are a few facts about donkeys in a biblical perspective to enhance your understanding and admiration to this friendly animal. It should be noted that God loves the donkey, as it is a popular animal mentioned in His book... the King James Version Bible.

BIBLICAL DONKEY FACTS

1. Donkeys are mentioned 140 times in the Bible (King James Version).
2. Samson used a jawbone of a donkey to kill 1,000 men. Read Judges 15:15
3. God made a donkey speak to a man. Read Numbers 22:21.
4. Jesus used a donkey in parables. Read Matthew 21:2, Luke 13:15 & 14:5.
5. Jesus rode a donkey. Read Zechariah 9:9 and John 12:14

HISTORICAL INTEREST

- The movie "How The West Was Won" was filmed here in Oatman, "Foxfire" and interestingly name that fits well for this area "Edge of Eternity."
- The donkeys of Oatman are the descendants of the old west prospectors.
- The Oatman donkeys are so famous busloads of people arrive just to meet, associate, dine with and have their picture taken with them. Photographs, T-shirts, coffee cups and other items honoring these "royalty" donkeys are for sale. They are honorable celebrities! However, it is not true that if you pet a donkey it will bring you good luck.

- The mines of Oatman produced about $40,000,00 in gold and some silver or 1.8 million ounces of gold multiplied by the price of gold today will give you its real monetary value. And there is more gold in the mountains yet to be found!
- Oatman was named in honor of Olive and Ann Oatman, wagon train emigrant children kidnapped by Indians, tattooed on the face and forced into slavery on February 18,1851. They were finally rescued by the U.S. army on February 28, 1856. There are books you can buy in Oatman telling the story.
- Clark Gable and Carol Lombard were married at Oatman Hotel March 29, 1939. Clark would often visit Oatman to play poker with the miners.
- The mines in the Lord's Mountain (Boundary Cone mine) produced the highest-grade ore of all the mines. The ore was so rich it was like great nuggets in the quartz. Special procedures had to be implemented to protect the ore. It was so rich the miners would have easily taken pieces home with them at the end of the shift. Source: Oatman Gold Mining Center a book by Roman Malachi 1975, page 35. Library of Congress card #75-18225.
- The Oatman Holy Land Tour was discovered in the last week of November 2003 by, James Russell. The tour book was completed in February 2004 and the print version was completed and published in February of 2006.

HOW THE HOLY LAND TOUR BEGAN

This Holy Land Tour location was first visited by me in November of 2002 but I did not recognize any of these Biblical scenes. I came to Laughlin, Nevada to spend the winter and for some unexplained reason I would stop my motorcycle and meet with the Lord at the north face of the Boundary Cone Mountain in Oatman, Arizona. It was a place to give thanks to God for everything and to present troubles for resolution. It was not a convenient place or a spectacular scenic location where anyone would normally stop, but I kept coming to this mountain (I now call it The Lord's Mountain). Why this mountain I did not know, but I would find out later that culminated in this book.

Preface

In 2003 it was my second winter to come here (I was not planning to spend the winter here. I wanted to go to Tucson or Phoenix, but I ended up here anyway). On my first visit this year (the last week of November 2003) to greet the Lord at the mountain, I looked up and I was shocked to discover a black cross etched into the north cliff of the volcano's cone. I never saw this last year and I was here many times the year prior. See Fig. 4 and 5 revealing this cross. It is actually a strong black shadow that can be seen from the north face of the volcanic cone. I have looked around in the canyons and I have not found anything like it. Before I give you directions to The Lord's Mountain I must tell you something else.

The next day I was on my way to return to the volcano taking Boundary Cone Road from the intersection of highway 95 in Mohave Valley, Arizona. I and many thousands of tourists and local residents have seen this cone too many times to count, but today as I drove by I looked up and what I saw was amazing. I had to stop to make sure I was seeing what was obvious. The shape of the Boundary Cone mountain as viewed from the west looking east was plain as day to see, it was the Lord sitting, wearing a flowing tunic, with his arms positioned as if circling whoever would stop by the north face of the mountain. Exactly where I would meet Him! See Fig. 1 and 2. This was starting to get my serious attention, but there is even more to the story!

A few days later in December 2003 I was lazily driving the canyon on my motorcycle and I stopped some distance away by a sandstone rock formation and saw what appeared as the ten commandment tablets etched into the side of a sandstone cliff. Then as I looked east I saw the huge Sphinx. This shocked me to see these formations that no one had recognized before. As I looked I found more Biblical references and I thought this was amazing that with more sites being discovered I should write a book so everyone who drives through old Route 66 can enjoy this unique scenic tour of the Holy Land in Oatman, Arizona.

Now I know why I was made to stop here in Oatman, Arizona at this mountain, it was God's mountain and it is here He revealed the obvious, yet hidden from our eyes, the wonderful Biblical mountain scenes. And

now it can be shared with all. Come see the Bible chiseled in stone!
– James Russell

....

The Oatman Arizona Holy Land Tour was discovered and the book produced by James Russell at age 51 who is shown in the photo Fig. A. The author's bike is a 2002 Harley Davidson Fat Boy motorcycle, 1,450 cc (or 88 cubic inch) motor. This motorcycle was used to view the sites, measure the miles and take photographs for this book.

THE AUTHOR

Fig. A / James Russell on Harley Davidson Fat Boy

ART GALLERY

For natural rock art photographic prints of Oatman and other areas of the nation come to JamesRussellPublishing. com You will see things you have never seen before!

Preface

THE MANY NAMES OF THE LORD

Many people do not realize that the Lord is a name for God, but also that He has many names! He is just too complex of a being to be narrowed down to just one description. Here's a list of names and a description of what His name means. You may use these names when you visit the Biblical sites to address Him when you speak to Him.

Just because the word Jehovah is used does not mean God is endorsing or is associated with the Jehovah Witness church denomination. The Bible was written long before they arrived.

1. Yahweh - God.
2. Jehovah- Self-existant one.
3. Jehovah Elohim - Lord God; strong, faithful and only true God.
4. Jehovah Jireh - The Lord will provide.
5. Jehovah Rapha - The Lord who heals.
6. Jehovah Nissi- The Lord our victor.
7. Jehovah Mekadiskem - The Lord our sanctifier.
8. Jehovah Shalom - The Lord our peace.
9. Jehovah Raah - The Lord our shepherd.
10. Jehovah Tsidkenu - The Lord our Righteousness.
11. Jehovah Shammah - The Lord is present.
12. Jehovah Sabaoth - The Lord of Hosts.
13. Adonai Jehovah - Lord God.
14. Jesus of Nazareth - Son of God.
15. Yeshua - Jesus.
16. Lord.

There are more names listed in the Bible. Consider using #1, #3, #4, #5, #11, #14, #15 and #16 when taking this tour.

CHAPTER 1

BEGIN TOUR #1

See Fig. 1. Notice the head and the flowing robe and encircling arms of the Lord. This is the Boundary Cone Mountain which is now called "The Lord's Mountain" Read Micah 4:1.

If you are not healed from an illness immediately it does not mean you will not be healed! God often will hear your request and grant it later. Some people's motives need to be tested while others need to repent of their wrongful behaviors and attitudes (sins) before they can be healed. The Lord is quick to forgive! Others need to simply stop resisting and doubting the Lord and let God heal them.

There are many books written by Christian organizations on how you can obtain healing from the Lord. They will help guide you. Once such easy to read booklet is, "Christ is the Divine Healer" published by Osterhus Publishing House, 4500 West Broadway, Minneapolis, Minnesota 55422. You can search for them also on the Web. They also have many tracts you should read then, if you wish, come back to the Lord's Mountain once again!

Tour #1

Note: Due to the narrow canyon and lack of parking and turnaround points on old Route 66 the tour will not be in logical Biblical historical time, but you will still enjoy the sights to see.

1. First visit is to the Boundary Cone volcano that is now called The Lord's Mountain! Get on Highway 95 on the Arizona side going south from Bullhead City, Arizona or North from Needles, California. Go east on Boundary Cone Road, the same way you normally would go to Oatman, Arizona. **Set your odometer to zero**. You will see the cone to the right side of the road about 3.5 miles ahead at the 2 o'clock position.

Fig. 1. The Lord's Mountain

Little did I know when I often came to speak to God at the bottom left corner of the photo beside the roadway not shown in the photograph that I was actually standing before this huge mountain between the arms of the Lord. It was shocking to me to see this one year later when I came back.

You can see this mountain from a great distance away from many points and it looks like the Lord sitting with hands on knees.

> ### *IDOL WORSHIPPING PROHIBITED*
> There is nothing holy to see or visit and nothing physical to worship as shrines, as doing such things are religious pagan activities, and not approved by God. Do not pray, bow or kneel down to the objects you see. But rather look to the unseen God who created all this and give Him your full attention. Remember the Ten Commandments says, #2 *"Thou shalt have no other Gods before me"* and #3 is *"Thou shalt not make unto thee any graven image, or any likeness of any thing that is in heaven above, or that is in the earth beneath, or that is in the water under the earth. Thou shalt not bow down thyself to them, nor serve them; for I the Lord thy God am a jealous God, visiting the iniquity of the fathers upon the children unto the third and fourth generation of them that hate me."* God does not take kindly to any form of idol worship, so don't do it, no matter who does.

I asked the Lord why I returned here again, then I saw the black cross in the mountain and then I saw this shape of the mountain. Those two messages were strong and led me to discover more Bible scenes nearby and lead to this book for you to enjoy.

To those who need to know Fig. 1 photo was taken ½ mile west of highway 95 on Boundary Cone Road.

2. Go 3.5 miles (heading east toward Oatman) and notice the mountain now looks like a lion. Amazingly, it will do this again as we go to the western south side of this wonderful mountain. The lion represents Jesus Christ, the Lion of the tribe of Judah. See Fig. 3. You may need to use a bit of imagination to help bring the image out. Later, with experience, you will see the lion.

Tour #1

Fig. 2. Wider View of The Lord's Mountain

Fig. 3. The Lord's Mountain / Lion of Tribe of Judah

Read Revelations 5:5. Examine Fig. 54 which is a view from the right side of this mountain and the Lion has turned around and now looking south. This is amazing! Not many mountains can duplicate themselves when viewed from different angles. If you look at other rock formations as you drive past them you will see them change shape, but never do they change shape to recreate an identical image of itself.

- Here in Fig. 2 the Lord's Mountain appears as a lion as viewed from the north and when viewed from the south it reverts back into a lion again! You can see this in Fig. 54.

3. When you get to the Route 66 intersection (Oatman Highway & Rt. 66) 4.4 miles ahead turn a right U-turn and go 1.0 mile to the Boundary Cone Mountain and park on the right side where the wash crosses the road (and hope a flash flood does not arrive, so park on the high side of the wash). Or just go 0.2 miles more and park in the small turnout where you can see the cross in the mountain much better with less walking.

Here you can meet with the Lord to give him thanks and make your requests known to Him. Read Exodus 15:26. Did you know the Lord wants you to call on Him in the day of trouble? Read Psalm 50:15.

- Fig. 5. is a wider view of the Lord's Mountain from where you are now standing.
- Fig. 5-A is photo of two large rocks that are the feet or footstools of the Lord. Read Matthew 5:35 and 22:44.
- Don't forget to use the names of the Lord you have learned.
- Do not be afraid to make your requests known to God.
- You can get a miracle right here at this very spot!

JESUS HEALS

This is a place for God's people to come to be anointed with oil and healing hands laid upon them, as prescribed in the Bible, and the sick shall be healed. Read James 5:14 and Psalm 30:2. Healing services may be performed here. Individuals may also come and appeal to Yahweh, Jesus of Nazareth for healing at any time! Read Isaiah 53:4.

Tour #1

Fig. 4. Cross In The Lord's Mountain

Dare to believe God will grant your request and keep believing it!

Fig. 5. Wider View of Fig. 4

The Lord is merciful and compassionate and He cares for You!

4. Walk across the road and you can roam about the gently sloping face of the cone. The black coating on the rocks is called desert varnish. It is created by weathering and mostly by the baking heat of the sun. Look up at the cliff and hear the silence or the swirling winds high above. It is a nice place to experience its majesty. You may see hawks nesting in the cliff and other birds. If you hear birds chirping it means they welcome you present your cares upon the Lord. Psalm 50:15 says, *"Call upon me in the day of trouble: I will deliver thee."* Read the entire Psalm so you will meet the "conditions" required for this wonderful promise to be realized.

5. Looking up at about the 3 o'clock position you should see a black cross. It is easy to see because the cone's rock is a soft red / white hue. If you still can't see it, then walk about 200 paces to your right (west) then look up and you will see it. If not, pray now for new eyes! See Fig. 4. Fig. 5 is a wider view. Fig. 5-B are Prayer Stones.

6. On the hillside to your left (east) not far away is an old gold mine. You can visit it and find beautiful frosted quartz crystals in veins near the mineshaft. Be careful not to fall into the deep vertical shaft, it will be a deadly fall! The tiny fine crystals look like white cake frosting or rock candy and will be found in the reddish color rocks in thin ribbon quartz veins.

- Did you notice there are other volcanic cones just to the southeast nearby? These cones represent the Apostles John, Peter the Rock and James. See Fig 6. From a more eastern location more of the Apostles will come into view. Feel free to discover and name these Apostles yourself.

DID YOU GET A MIRACLE?
If you received a miracle we would like to know about it to share the good news. Contact JamesRussellPublishing.com.

Tour #1

Fig. 5-A. The Lord's Mountain / Footstools or Feet

Fig. 5-B. Prayer Stones

- Before you leave, and if you have prayed to the Lord a special request, triple stack three stones as shown in Fig. 5-B. Any size stones will be fine. The three stones represent God the Father, God the Son and God the Holy Ghost and it "seals" your prayer request to the Lord. It does not matter if the stack withstands weather conditions, it is a sign between you and the Lord and He will see it forever and ever in His heart. You can triple stack stones at any of the site locations where you have prayed a special request to the Lord.

- Take a photograph of your prayer stack of stones for memories and to remind you of your prayer and your act of faith. You may want to hang the picture in your home or keep it in your wallet as a reminder. However, if you find yourself praying to the picture, it is becoming an idol. Burn it (in a safe place) and present the ashes to the Lord!

ASK YOURSELF

How many times have you traveled this road and have never seen these amazing rock formations? Reading this book will give you "artistic eyes" so you can see and discover even more no matter where you go! This new talented gift will last a lifetime.

Fig. 6. The Apostles

YOUR APPOINTMENT WITH GOD

Never pray to the mountain for the Lord condemns idols. Just meet Him here. You can leave a prayer request on paper under a rock so it will not blow away in the wind. Read Psalm 50:15 for a very strong promise from the Lord! Read Deuteronomy 5:7. Answer to prayer or healing can be instant or gradual. Be firm in your faith and "believe" in God's promises to deliver you.

Tour #1

- If you look to the far northeast you can see Noah's Ark sitting on the side of the tall mountain, Mt. Ararat. It is slopping downward, left to right, and it looks like a long black train. Can you see the ark shape now? A huge box shape hull of an old brown or black wood ship? If not, we will visit it later when we get closer to it. See Fig. 9 so you can recognize it.
- If you walk west along the road to the road sign that says, "Do not enter when flooded" go 19 paces east, then 35 paces south to a large split rock you can sit on. On a calm or a windy day you may hear the sound of rushing water. The Lord's voice is like mighty waters or can be a soft whisper.

> *The Bible says to cry to the Lord for deliverance from your affliction. Read Psalm 30:2*

7. Drive back toward Oatman and go 0.5 miles and look right (south) and you will see the deep Valley of the Shadow of Death. People with RV's do dry camp here. See Fig. 7. Read Psalm 23:4.

Fig. 7. Valley of the Shadow of Death

You can see the valley walls closing in on you! The valley extends way back into the far mountains and continues on to the east and west. It is a multitude of valleys interconnected to form a maze. A bad place to get lost in.

8. At the Y-intersection go 0.6 miles and park. Here you can see the "Rock of Ages." This is the Rock of Ages and a high tower of protection. Fig. 8. Read II Samuel 23:3. All the minor peaks to your left and right are life's troubles, but the Lord stands above these. Read Psalm 9-9 and 18:2. Many are the afflictions of the righteous but the Lord delivers him from them all. Read Psalm 34:19 and 9:9. Also read Isaiah 41:10.

Fig. 8. Rock of Ages

A miracle can happen here at this location, so be prepared to make your request known to Him. If your faith is weak then ask God for His faith to make it happen!

The Rock of Ages looks like a person sitting on a throne with both arms on the throne's armrests. You can see this better in person as it requires a three dimentional experience to fully appreciate this rock formation.

> *Be Still, and know that I am God... Psalm 46:10*

9. Go 0.5 miles and park. Here you can see again Noah's Ark, see Fig. 9 in center of photo.

- The Ark is the large dark wall-like formation in the center of Fig. 9. Read Genesis 8:4. There is another similar formation below it. It would be interesting to say the one below was an attempt of other people to escape with Noah by also building a ship, but they were too late. Of course this is not in the Bible, but there are many instances in the Bible where those who scoff at God never escape destruction.

Fig. 9. Noah's Ark

- Lot's Wife is the white peak in Fig. 10.
- Now go to downtown Oatman to start tour #2 and #3. They have many Biblical scenes you do not want to miss.
- As you drive into Oatman, keep looking to your right (east) and you will see the ruins of the Temple of Jerusalem. See Fig. 10-A. The top level is the Temple Mount!

Fig. 10. Lot's Wife - A Pillar of Salt

Fig. 10-A. King Solomon's Temple

CHAPTER 2

BEGIN TOUR #2

10. **Reset your odometer to zero** in front of the Oatman Hotel.

11. Leaving Oatman, heading north out of town, at 0.3 miles stop and park. To your left (west) is a hole in the rock peak. This is where Jesus spoke saying it is easier for a man to pass through the eye of a needle than a rich man to enter heaven. (Luke 18:25.) (He meant the love and hoarding of money for selfish purpose, not having money for even Joseph of Arimathaea was rich and Jesus' disciple. See Fig. 11. Read Isaiah 53:9 and Matthew 27:57.

Fig. 11. Eye of the Needle

12. Go 3.0 miles and park. This is the Gates of Hell. See Fig. 12. You don't want to go to hell. Today is the day of salvation! Read Luke 19:9.

Fig. 12. Gates of Hell

13. At 0.5 miles (almost 0.6 miles) park and you will see something amazing. This is the cave Jesus was buried in. The tomb is not deep, but it is best not to go inside as it could collapse. If you are looking for Jesus, He is not there. It is empty because He Is Risen! He's Alive!

- Note that there are very few trees of life growing here and nowhere else for miles around. They stand in testimony that the Lord has eternal life to all who come to Him. See Fig. 13. Read John 3:15.

- Fig. 13-A is a first look at eternal life. A view from Jesus' tomb.

Fig. 13. Jesus' Empty Tomb by the Tree of Life

Fig. 13-A / First View of Eternal Life

Tour #2

14. Go 1.2 miles and park. On the right you will see steps chiseled in the stone leading up to where Moses struck The Rock in Horeb with his staff and water to this day still drips from this rock. See. Fig. 14. Read Exodus 17:1.

Fig. 14 / The Rock of Horeb

- Fig. 14-a is water overflowing from Moses Rock in Horeb Spring. Running water is a rare sight to see in these desert mountains. The Lord keeps his promises. To this day wild donkeys visit to drink water from the crack in this rock. They also drink at the Garden of Eden in Fig. 17-E.

Fig. 14-A / Running Water at Rock of Horeb

- Fig. 14-B is a surprise. A refreshing pool of water with live goldfish living in it.

Fig. 14-B / Moses Rock with Wild Goldfish

15. Go 0.5 miles and look north to the yellow sandstone cliffs, just left of the cave opening you can see written in stone ancient Hebrew writings of the Old Testament Bible. See Fig. 14-C. If you look about the entire length of the yellow sandstone cliffs as you take this tour you will see more writings. There is no place to park here, but you can see this again on the return trip by Temptation Cliffs. See Fig. 26.

Fig. 14-C / Ancient Writing

16. Go 3.5 miles and when the road flattens out we will turn left to enter the Back Country Byway Desert Information center. See Fig. 14-D. Someday there may be a real information center here with full amenities! Maybe a State or National Park! Look west and you will see the foundation of the Tower of Babylon. There is a spiral staircase leading up to the foundation. See Fig. 14-E. Read Genesis 11:4.

Fig. 14-D / Desert Information Center

Fig. 14-E / Tower of Babylon

- Note that sunlight and shadows change in the seasons. I saw these formations in winter and spring morning and afternoon, but afternoon 1pm to 4 pm I found lighting was best when east of Sitgreaves Pass. A local guide may or may not be needed in the summer months to see the sites if light or shadows obscure some formations.

- Notice the tall peak in background. This is actually the Great Sphinx of Egypt, but it does not even look like it at all from this angle. Compare the photo in Fig. 24 with this photo Fig. 14-D to witness a great and wonderful transformation!

- Read the notices on the bulletin board. If you plan to go off road, it would be wise to post a notice here of when you expect to return. It may be helpful.

- We recommend that you not leave the paved road in this tour except to visit this Desert Information Center. This part of the desert is a very dangerous place with many deep ravines, rattlesnakes, coyotes and sometimes wild dogs. The desert is hot, dry and without water you will dehydrate rapidly.

FORGIVENESS

There is a big secret of getting healed from a disease and it is boiled down to one word... forgiveness. You must forgive those who have wronged you. I once forgave a person who gave me a spinal injury and the Lord healed me of the infirmity the moment I did so. I was amazed at this and I still am.

So, when you stand before the Lord at any of these mountain places remember to tell Him that you forgive those whom have hurt you. Now ask the Lord to be merciful upon you, as you have been merciful to them who have hurt you.

God has His ways that mercy begets mercy. If you are merciful He too will be merciful to you. Fair and square!

17. To see the "Devil on the Run" pull out from the Information Center and go east 0.3 miles, park the vehicle and look to the north and you will see a huge boulder with horns racing up the side of the mountain leaving a white trail of dust. You can't miss it.

It is very unique and impressive to see a rock that looks like a devil with horns, but is running so fast up the mountain its feet are tearing up the stones and gravel behind it.

There is no other rock formation like this one in any of our National Parks. See Fig. 14-F. Do you know why he is on the run? KJV Bible verse: *"Resist the devil, and he will flee from you."* - James 4:7.

Fig. 14-F / Devil on the Run

18. **Drive back to the Desert Information Center and Reset your odometer to zero.** Now we can go back up the canyon (heading west).

CHAPTER 3

BEGIN TOUR #3

19. At 0.5 miles you will see an old gas station. This was Cool Springs a Route 66 landmark. It is not Biblical, but noteworthy to point out. The book, "The Grapes of Wrath" will give you an idea how hard it was to travel this road you are now on. See Fig. 15. (The author's 2002 Harley Davidson Fat Boy motorcycle is between the gasoline pumps). In the background you can see the Great Sphinx beginning to take shape.

Fig. 15 / Historic Rt. 66 / Cool Springs

- The road you are on is Route 66 and it extends from Chicago to Los Angeles. It is slowly being rebuilt as a tourist attraction after many years of abandonment. There is a publication called Route 66 Magazine and books you can buy describing this historical highway.

20. Go 0.7 miles and park. Look northwest. These are the foundation stones of a huge furnace. See Fig. 16. This furnace was so hot it burned to death the soldiers who tended the fire, but the three men of God tossed into the furnace did not burn. There was also a fourth person who was not thrown into that raging inferno seen walking about the flames who was like the Son of God . Read Daniel 3:14.

Fig. 16 / Furnace Foundations

21. Go 1.0 miles and park. You can see the great Sphinx to the east. If you can't find it we will see it again later. Try to locate it on your own! If you have visited this area before ask yourself why you missed seeing this huge Sphinx? It was never hidden from view. Isn't it plain to see? It is as if the Lord sealed our eyes from seeing any of these formations. This is the first miracle of The Oatman Holy Land Tour! Now everybody sees and it is a huge tourist attraction. We will show a picture of this Sphinx later.

22. Go 0.6 miles, stop and park. Look to the north and down and you will see a small forest of four trees, but extremely huge trees for this desert! This is the Garden of Eden! The four trees also can represent the four rivers in the Garden of Eden; Pison, Gihon, Hiddekel and Euphrates in Geneses 2:14. See Fig. 17. (photo taken about 0.1 miles west of here looking east). Read Genesis 2:8 and 3:24. You can walk down paths here and see streams and pools of water (at least in the winter).

- Residences may be nearby and the Garden of Eden may even be on private property in the future, so do not trespass, if posted.

Fig. 17-A is a tree that is full of long thorns. It resembles the Crown of Thorns Jesus wore on the way to the crucifixion. Fig. 17-B is a closer view.

Fig. 17-A / Tree of Thorns

Fig. 17-B / Tree of Thorns (closer view)

- Fig. 17-C. reveals the immense size of the trunk of the cottonwood trees here. There are two big trees and two smaller ones. Note the running water behind the tree. It is no wonder they have thrived. What is amazing is you will have to drive a hundred miles or more to see a tree this big in the middle of this desert! These very rare monsters only grow wild here in the Garden of Eden!

Fig. 17-C / Tree of Life in the Garden of Eden

- Fig. 17-D is a beautiful photograph of the Cottonwood tree growing in the Garden of Eden. You can get an idea just how huge this tree is growing in a desert where for a hundred miles or more no tree exists, but here it is! Can you see the hawk's nest in the tree? This photo was taken in the winter months of February, 2004. It was about 60 degrees... cold for the desert! Read Mark 4:30.

> To Appreciate this Garden of Eden you need to realize we are in a harsh desert and for running water and huge trees to exist here are precious scenes to behold. You will not see this for many hundreds of miles in any direction, not even near the mighty Colorado River! This is a very special place.

Fig. 17-D / Tree of Life in the Garden of Eden

- The running stream in Fig. 17-E is in the Garden of Eden. The trees are watered by the River of Life. Read Revelation 22:1.

Fig. 17-E / Running Stream in the Garden of Eden

- Notice the new branches look like an Aspen or Birch tree. See Fig. 17-F. As if one seed had somehow fallen onto the Cottonwood tree branch, sprouted and the seedling tapped into the Cottonwood branch and grew. In any case, look around, drive for miles and you will not see trees this type or size. It is here for you to enjoy! Only these rare trees you find right here in the Garden of Eden! Read John 15:1.

Fig. 17-F / New Branch on the Tree of Life

- This is a fine place to stop and rest. Please remove any trash that you may see laying around, even if it is not yours. Your kindness will be appreciated!

- Be mindful it is possible that mosquitoes, serpents and other critters may be present.

- Climb out of the Garden of Eden back to the road. Look south to the broken pinnacle at the top of the mountain. This is the shattered remains of a statue of a false god that Hezekiah broke in the high places. See Fig. 18.
- You can see a better view if you walk east to see the eastern side where you can see broken pieces of the statue that has tumbled down the mountain side. See Fig. 18-A. Read Deuteronomy 12:2 and II Chronicles 34:7.

23. Go 0.1 miles and look right (east) as you make the turn for a good view of the Garden of Eden. There is no place to park here. See Fig. 17.

Fig. 18 / Broken Statue

God really does hate some things and one of the things he truly dispises is idols. Read the second of the Ten Commandments.

Fig. 18-A / Broken Statue (east view)

Thou shalt not make unto thee any graven image. If you have idols in your car, motorcycle or in your home you need to get rid of them! The Lord means business when it comes to idol worship and He will not hear the prayers of those who break His commands and think nothing of it.

24. As you drive up the road on the right you will see Ed's Camp. This is not Biblically historical, but there is something living here that should not be here! It is that extremely huge Saguaro cactus about thirty feet tall. This is the only one a hundred miles or more where they grow to such immense size in the wild. It is the unusual gigantic size of this cactus that makes it special. It has holes in it for birds to nest in. In any event, you just don't see huge cactus like this in this mountainous zone of Arizona, but interestingly, here you can. It looks like a person clapping hands! See Fig. 18-AA. Read Psalm 47:1.

Fig. 18-AA / Broken Statue (east)

25. Pharaoh's Mummy or Adam. In front of Ed's Camp look north following the outline of the hilltop against the sky and you will see a remarkable image of a man laying down (his head is to your left).

Fig. 18-B / Adam

He is lying just left (west) to the great Sphinx of Egypt. See Fig. 18-B. Or perhaps it is not Pharaoh and it is Adam of the Bible created from the dust of the earth! KJV Bible verse: Genesis 2:7 *"And the Lord God formed man of the ground and breathed into his nostrils the breath of life and man became a living soul."*

- **Fact:** The word Egypt can be found 646 times in the Bible! Today books and movies reveal the curse of the mummy and other Egyptian tales. But God has put a real curse on Egypt, nations and individuals. He said in Genesis 12:3 *"And I will bless them that bless thee, and curse him that curses thee..."*. Egypt was a formidable and powerful nation in the world, but because it cursed and enslaved the Jews it is less than a whimper in the world of nations ever since God said through Moses to Pharaoh, *"Let my people go!"*
- If you follow history, you can see this curse is alive and well. The sun never set on England's kingdom for it was great in size, but when they opposed and betrayed the Jews to settle in Jerusalem, England is now a crumbling kingdom. Fabulous Rome and Egypt mistreated Jews and today they are a pile of ruins only tourists visit. Hitler mistreated the Jews and Germany never dominated the world. Africa rejected Israel becoming a nation and is under God's curse and is now suffering greatly. The Bible is true after all!

- Is the United States betraying Israel? We may very well be by selling advanced weapon systems to the Arabs who will use these weapons on Israel. Selling weapons to Israel's traditional enemies is certainly not an act of blessing Israel. We are raising our hand against Israel. If this does not cease terrible troubles will arise. God says so in His Bible.
- The Bible is a powerful book because what it says happens! Malachi 3:10 reveals a financial curse on those who rob God. There are also many "blessings" revealed in the Bible. Read them!

26. Go 0.2 miles and park. Look to the north at the 12 o'clock position and you will see a very high mountain shaped like a stepped Pyramid. This is Mt. Zion where God himself resides and people are not to come near it. This is why it is set so far back from the road. See Fig. 19. Read Psalm 125:1 and 3:4.

Fig. 19 / Mt. Zion

27. Look below in the yellow sandstone cliff to see the Book of Life. See Fig. 20. Read Revelation 20:12. The rock has vertical cracks where you can see about four books as on a bookshelf. It is here God has recorded everything you've ever thought, said or did. Make sure your name is written in these books. Your name must appear in the Book of Life to get into heaven. There is no alternative! The Bible gives a clear warning if your name does not appear you will not get into heaven, but you will be thrown into a lake of fire. See Fig. 29.

Fig. 20 / Books of Life

YOUR FIRST INTRODUCTION

This may be the first time you have ever been introduced to the Lord of the Bible. Maybe you saw movies, but this time you are getting a front row seat in a personal first-hand living experience, something you will remember for the rest of your life.

People may try to convince you otherwise and talk you out of getting your miracle, but do not let the unbelievers cheat you out of what God wants to give to you. God keeps His promises. All you have to do is find them in the Bible which is not hard to do for there are over 800 promises. You only need a handful, if that! Go buy a King James Version Bible, read it and believe it!

28. At 3 o'clock you can see the Ten Commandments The first two on the left is the Old Testament Commandments and the third tablet on the right is the New Testament Command to obey the commands of Jesus. (Read the Bible to discover these commands) Exodus 20:1. If you can't see them, you may see them up ahead at another stop.

Fig. 21 / Ten Commandments & Two Faces

- There are three weatherworn tablets or two depending on the angle of the sun on the face of the rock in the right side panel. See Fig. 21. Read Exodus 34:28. It is best viewed when the sun is on a slight angle casting a slight shadow in the tablets. Late afternoon around 4 pm is good.
- From different points of view in the canyon you can see the Ten Commandments better or worse due to shifting shadows. Some angles it will look like two tablets and some angles reveal three tablets.
- There are two ways to see the Ten Commandments. You can see two small tablets in one panel as in Fig. 21 or simply see two panels as being the whole. It does look like writing on both of the large panels.

- If you look closely at Fig. 21 you will see the profiles of two persons. They are both facing to the right, one behind the other.

Fig. 22 / Jesus Cave

29. At 9 o'clock position is the cave where Jesus slept in the wilderness. See Fig. 22. Read Luke 9:58. Do you see faces in the rock?

- Just below the cave is the Mount of Olives. We will see this up ahead in the tour.

Fig. 23 / Mt. Carmel

20. To the east is a black mound of volcanic rocks. This is Mt. Carmel were Elijah called down fire from heaven. See Fig. 23. Kings 18:17.

31. Go 0.2 miles and park. A good view of 10 Commandments, Mt. Zion, Mount of Olives, Broken Statue and Mt. Carmel. See Fig. 24 for a view of the Great Sphinx of Egypt. If you have traveled Rt. 66 often ask yourself why you have never saw this before? It is obviously huge and can't be missed! Look at the detail of the sitting cat (Sphinx).

Fig. 24 / The Great Sphinx

32. Go 0.3 miles and park. Here you can see the Ten Commandments to the north-east, The Book of Life, Mount of Olives and Mt. Zion.

- If you look east (back down the canyon) you will see the Great Sphinx of Pharaoh who refused to allow the Jews to escape from Egypt. The big Valley in the distant east is Megiddo, where Armageddon takes place Read Revelation 16:16.
- Turn this page to the left to landscape view and cover the protrusion of rock in the upper-left with your finger. The face of Moses appears. Look for the chin, lips and eye.

- At the foot of the sandstone cliffs is a small canyon where John the Baptist preached and baptized in water. See Fig. 25. Read Luke 3:1. Jesus was baptized in water by John at this location. Read John 1:9.

Fig. 25 / John Baptist Canyon

- Can you see Temptation Cliffs where Jesus fasted for 40 days and nights and was tempted by the devil? (Matthew 4:11) It is all along the top of the yellow sandstone formation. The devil tempted Jesus to jump off these cliffs because God would protect his fall. Jesus resisted and rebuffed the devil using the Word of God. See Fig. 26. Read Matthew 4:1.
- Note again the cave where Jesus slept in the wilderness.

Fig. 26 / Temptation Cliffs

- To the left you can see the ancient Hebrew writings of the Old Testament chiseled in stone. We saw this earlier coming down the mountain.

- On top of this cliff to the left (northwest) is a small mountain peak visible. This is the high mountain where the devil showed Jesus all the kingdoms of the world to be given to him if only Jesus would worship the devil. No deal transpired. See Fig. 26. Read Matthew 4:5.

- At the 3 o'clock position you should see the Mount of Olives (or the Garden of Gethsemane read John 18:1). Amazingly, the perimeter rocks of the garden have formed the shape of a heart. Plants grow here appear as distant olive trees. See Fig. 27. Read Matthew 21:1, 24:3 and 26:30. This could also be the Garden of Gethsemane?

Fig. 27 / Mount of Olives / A Perfect Heart

33. Go 0.2 miles and look north for an excellent head-on view of the Mt. of Olives. There is no place to stop here.

34. Go about 100 feet and park. See Fig. 28. The rocks are burnt because the Lake of Fire is here and they are twisted from the torment of flames.

Fig. 28 / Opal Mines

OPAL MINE

The brown volcanic lava rocks in the foreground about you are opal mines (yes brilliant fire opals can be found here). The opals are soft milky white veins. The rocks are mostly red in color, but look closely and you will see what looks like grains of quartz. There are no quartz veins here. What you see are opals. As you look around and become more experienced to identify opal veins you will find large opals as big as your thumb, or larger with ease. Most of them will not be fire opals, just clear opals. There are thousands of veins in the rocks here so look closely and you will see them. You may need a rock pick to break the rocks encasing the veins of opals. There are many more opal mine areas nearby and alongside the road for easy pickings. The fire is in brown opals and visible when polished. Do not trespass on posted mining claims!

35. Walk north a few feet and you will come to an abrupt cliff. This pit is the Lake of Fire where angels will push those whose names are not in the Book of Life into a flaming pool of fire. You do not want to go here. See Fig. 29. Read Revelation 21:8. Read Luke 16:19 that speaks of another Lazarus who escaped this hell.

Fig. 29 / Lake of Fire

- Keep in mind Jesus did not mean being rich sent the rich man to hell, but the rich man was so caught up with his money he neglected mercy and compassion toward others.

A GAMBLE NOT WORTH TAKING

There are those who scoff at a place of eternal suffering called hell, but regardless if you do not believe in it you are still going there, forever and ever if your name is not in the Lambs Book of Life. You will spend billions of years in hell. Why take such a chance? Accept God's way of salvation and save yourself from eternal destruction. Heaven is a better place and all it takes is a simple decision to get there! Read John 3:16.

HELL IS:	
A lake of fire; Revelation. 20:15	Where there is no rest; Revelation 14:11
A bottomless pit; Revelation: 20:1	Where they wail; Mathew 13:42
A place of weeping; Matthew 8:12	A place of sorrows; Psalm 18:5
A furnace of fire; Mathew 13:41	A place of outer darkness; Matthew 25:30
A place of torments; Luke 16:23	A horrible tempest; Psalm 11:6
Where they scream for mercy; Luke 16:24	Where they never repent; Matthew 12:32
Everlasting punishment; Matthew 25:46	Where God is cursed; Revelation 16:11
Where they gnaw their tongues. Rev. 16:10	Feel the wrath of God; Revelation 14:10
Place of everlasting destruction; 2Thes. 1:9	For devil and his angels; Matthew 25:41
Place of everlasting burnings; Isaiah 33:14	The fire never goes out; Mark 9:48
They scream for mercy; Luke 16:24	Where they do not want their loved ones to go; Luke 16:28

....

ARE YOU GOING TO HELL?

God does not send people to hell; they send themselves by rejecting the Savior (Read John 3:16). At the judgment there will be a judge (Jesus of Nazareth). There will be a prosecution but no defense and a sentence with no appeal. There will be no second chance because the Bible says today is the day of salvation and if you reject Jesus Christ today you will hear these words on judgment day, *"Depart from me, you cursed, into the everlasting fire prepared for the devil and his angels."* Tough words but you can read it for yourself in Matthew 25:41. God means what He says!

- If you look north you will see a stepped pyramid, which is Mt. Zion. Interestingly, the Lord's dwelling place is in the north. Read Psalm 48:2.

Fig. 30 / Mt. Zion

- Another interesting note is the Bible said the north section of the sky was vacant and astronomers have discovered a vacant area of space in the north absent of stars and galaxies. The world is also hanging on nothing in space. Read Job 26:7.
- Satan desired to ascent above the stars of God and sit in the sides of the north. Read Isaiah 13:14.
- Read Ezekiel 1:4 what he saw coming out of the north.
- Look north in the night sky by the north pole and you will see where God resides in heaven. The Bible says it is so.

36. As you drive up the road before the next location you can see a gap in the red rocks. This is a narrow gate to heaven. The Bible says that few will enter heaven. So if you are following the crowd, you need to evaluate your true standing with the Lord. No photo taken.

SYMPTOMS

Look not at your illness or predicament symptoms that you suffer from, but look to the Word of God. For what He has promised He will deliver. Read Christian books on how to obtain healing and deliverance from God. At the back of this book we list some ministries that have such books. If you truly want to be made whole again... read the Bible and believe what you read!

Fig. 31 / David's Cave

37. Go 0.2 miles you will see a rough landscape of David's Wilderness to the west. Nearby you will see a cave in the red color rocks, see Fig. 31. This is the cave where David prayed to the Lord for protection from King Saul. The roof has caved in. Read Psalm 142:1.

38. Go 0.1 miles. The ridges you see is Barabbas Cliffs where Barabbas and his band of zealots attacked the Romans but lost the battle and he was jailed awaiting execution. See Fig. 32. Read Mark 15:7 and Luke 23:19-25.

WHAT IS A TITHE?

A tithe is the giving to the Lord 10% of your gross wages to put food on His table and He will put food on your table in return and much more! Read Malachi 3:10.

There is no temple today to give your tithes to, so you need to take your tithe money and invest it yourself; in your own ministry to bring forth good fruit to the Lord. He wants the lost to be saved. That is where you spend your tithe money... wherever the lost is being saved and the best way to insure that you are on the right track is to buy Gospel tracts and leave them everywhere you go. Do this and you cannot go wrong!

Fig. 32-A / Barabbas' Cliffs

39. Go 0.7 miles up the canyon and stop to see the rock at Kadesh. Here you can see the split rocks where God told Moses to speak to the rock to obtain water, but Moses struck the rock with anger. God kept his promise and the rocks split and gushed water from the cracks, but Moses was not allowed to enter the Promised Land for this act of disobedience. Fig. 33 reveals two vertical cracks in the rock from top to bottom that gushed the waters of Meribah. Read Numbers 20:11, 20:13 and 20:27. (You can see Moses standing alone gazing at the Promised Land in tour # 3, Fig. 50). If you look at the center rock it has the Face of the Devil. It resembles a bull with a distorted and mean looking human appearance.

- In the Bible, the Lord made water flow from a rock twice. It required millions of gallons of water to serve the needs of about three million of people in the desert.

TESTING YOUR ARTISTIC EYE

In Fig. 32-A can you make out a profile of a face? A face is forming on the right side of the cliff's edge located upper left in the photograph. It is not perfectly defined, but a face is clearly being chisseled in stone little-by-little each year. If you look at the shadows on the rock face another face will appear with a round open mouth as if he is calling for you.

Fig. 33 / Rock of Kadesh

- Can you see any faces in Fig. 33? Look and keep on looking. You may see some.
- Hint: the rock segment on the left is an entire head with eyes and mouth and even a mop of hair. He is looking at you! Now do you see?
- The rock segment in the middle has a very montrous distorted face like a demon. The rock segment on the far right has a very small face two eyes and a mouth with large lips. She is looking at the other two guys with wary eyes!
- When you see a rock with holes in it look for faces that can be formed in the rock. Look for the eyes and mouth first, then ears.
- With practice you will develop "artistic eyes" to recognize these hidden images.
- In time you will get better at it!
- It is a skill that needs to be learned.
- It is like looking for the Man in the Moon for the first time. At first you don't see it, then suddenly he comes into view!
- You are already learning by taking this tour.

40. Go up the canyon 0.4 miles to the top of Sitgreaves Pass and park. You can see a lot of what we have covered so far. You are now 3550 feet above sea level. See Fig. 34. Read Isaiah 60:2.

Fig. 34 / Sitgreaves Pass - Looking East

WHEN DOUBT STRIKES

You can be certain doubt will slip into your thoughts, all sorts of doubts to get you to not believe God's Word as it is written in the Bible. Even well meaning religious people will be stumbling blocks to you, if you listen to them and not to the Lord.

Whenever you doubt seek out the promise of God and hold on tight to it saying, "Thus said the Lord, it is written..."

Give thanks to God not for the trial or illness, but give Him thanks for His mercy, for His Word and for His deliverance. He has the power to deliver you and to create a miracle if need be to get the job done. Your job is to not give up and simply keep on believing God's Word to deliver you. Be stubborn in your faith!

Remember to be merciful to others and to get to work to proclaim the Gospel to the lost. No slackers needed!

41. Go 0.2 miles (heading west) down the mountain toward Oatman, and park. Walk north a few steps and you will see on the adjacent hillside to the left (looking northwest) rocks on a flat surface that resemble the foundation ruins of the Judgment Hall where Jesus met Pontius Pilate. A mock trial took place of gross injustice. See Fig. 35. Read John 18:28 and 19:13.

Fig. 35 / Judgment Hall

42. Look to the north and you will notice a rock that looks like a crown. This is where Jesus was crowned by Roman soldiers with a crown of thorns. See Fig. 36. Read Mark 15:17.

Fig. 36 / A Crown for a King

43. Look to the right (north-east) and you will see red stones scattered about the ground. This is Golgotha, the Place of the Skull where Jesus was crucified. The stones are still wet from his red blood shed for you. See Fig. 37. Read John 19:16. Of course a black & white photo will not show the red stains.

Fig. 37 / Blood Soaked Stones

44. Can you see the skull of Golgotha? It is just below Pilate's Judgment Hall in Fig 35. The skull is in the face of the rock in the lower left. See close-up view in Fig. 38. This is the place of the skull. Read Mark 15:22.

Fig. 38 / Golgotha the Skull

- Consider the odds of all three of these scenes in Fig. 35, 36 and 37 to be within a few feet of each other. Where else is there a skull in the rocks? Only here.

- You can walk west to the overlook for a great view of the Colorado river valley below, but this is also a cemetery and ashes of loved ones are sprinkled about the rocks, so please be respectful to this place. The author has opted not to photograph this precious ground in deep respect to the deceased and their surviving families.

45. Going down the mountain at 0.3 miles slow down and look left and you will see the tomb opening where Jesus was buried. We saw this earlier in Fig. 13.

46. At 0.5 miles you can park to see the Gates of Hell we saw earlier in Fig. 12, but just ahead looking to the west is a pile of rocks on the side of a hill. It is just one of King Solomon's Mines. The mines are spread out everywhere in these mountains. See Fig. 39. Read Haggai 2:8.

Fig. 39 / King Solomon's Mine

Okay it really isn't King Solomon's Mine, but it is a vertical mine shaft from the days of the old west.

47. Go 0.6 miles to the entrance to the Gold Road Mine. They have a restaurant, gift shop and gold mine tour. The tour may not exist if the mine is put back into operation. There is still more gold to be retrieved in this mine. It is currently the deepest and largest mine in Oatman. See Fig. 40.

Fig. 40 / Gold Road Gold Mine

PROSPECTING TIP

There's gold in the hills, but most is low grade, but don't let that fool you. A high grade vien is still likely to exist. Use a black light (ultraviolet light) to shine on quartz. If the quartz glows a sickly pale yellow color you have found gold ore!

48. Go 0.5 miles and park. Look north and you will see The Judgment Seat of Christ. Read Revelation 20:4. Some people will call it the Great White Throne. Read Revelation 20:11. See Fig. 41.

EMPLOYMENT OPPORTUNITY

Looking for a job? The Lord is hiring! Go to our Christian Website JamesRussellPublishing.com and look for the article "employment opportunity." All ages are welcome!

- Notice the cup-shaped rock to the left. This is the anvil Jesus will use when He slams down the gavel in judgment! To the right is a notch in the mountain that looks like a narrow gate to heaven. Will you enter this gate? Read Matthew 7:14. The red rock spires below are the four and twenty elders. Read Revelation 4:4.

Fig. 41 / Judgment Seat of Christ / Anvil and Elders

49. To the left where you parked (east) is a high mountain and valley sealed with no escape. This place is where the fiery serpents came from. You may not want to walk around this place if you are not right with God. Moses was on top of this mountain peak holding up a serpent of brass on a pole. We know serpents (rattlesnakes) live here, so be careful. The top of the cliff undulates like a serpent. In the photograph the snake's head is to the left, body is center and tail to the right. See Fig. 42. Read Numbers 21:6. The Lord does not honor those who murmur (complain) about Him for not taking care of business and not providing. Do not murmur!

Fig. 42 / Valley of the Serpent

50. "Angel Guarding the Sides of the North of Mt. Zion." Huge, but distant white angel can be seen. Go 0.5 miles from the Valley of the Serpents and park. Look north and you will see a huge angel (there are actually two angels, but only the larger one is shown in this photo). They are hard to see due to distance. These are the only formations far away as most formations are relatively close to the roadside and are easy to see.

These angel formations are eerie to observe out in the deep wilderness. They stand strong-willed in a harsh dismal landscape! See. Fig. 42-A. KJV Bible verse: *"Beautiful for situation, the joy of the whole earth, is mount Zion, on the sides of the north, the city of the great King."* - Psalm 48:2. You can see the angel with the naked eye. Look for a sharp pinnacle with broad wings standing. It is looking to the left.

Note: The Angel is actually located near highway 68 just above Bullhead City near Laughlin, Nevada. It is often called Finger Rock or some other names I will not mention here. From this angle and point of view in Oatman the rock formation does look like a huge angel.

Tour #3

Fig. 42-A / Guardian Angel

51. Go 1.5 miles you will see a tall blonde pinnacle rock protruding out of the darker mountain. Traditionally it is called Elephant Tooth rock, but for this book it is Lot's wife, turned into a pillar of salt. She is looking south toward Sodom and Gomorrah. See Fig. 43. You can see Lot's Wife in the extreme left in Fig. 44. Read Genesis 19:26. Fig. 44 is a wide view containing the Biblical scenes of Fig. 43, 44, 45 and 46.

Fig. 43 / Lot's Wife - A Pillar of Salt

- If you look closely at Fig. 65 you can see what appears as a standing woman facing you set inside a pillar of salt. The white color rock is actually not salt, but a volcanic rock.

Fig. 44 / Oatman Mountains

52. Just beyond Lot's Wife to the south is a rock formation with a central figure, the Lord Jesus, and surrounding it are spires that represent the apostles Peter, James, John and his brother with Moses and Elias. This is the Transfiguration Mountain. See Fig. 45. Read Matthew 17:1.

Fig. 45 / Transfiguration Rock

Fig. 45 looks like people standing around a tall rock.

53. And just to the south of this rock is another that looks similar, but it is a group of people crowding in on Jesus. A sick woman touches the hem of Jesus garment and is healed. The scene is frozen in stone. See Fig. 46. Read Mark 5:25.

Fig. 46 / Woman Healed

54. Go on into Oatman, find a place to park and walk about the town and get a bite to eat before we head out again.

Fig. 64 Gunfighters in Oatman

55. Fig. 47 is a photo of downtown Oatman looking south. Author's motorcycle is in the right foreground. Oatman is a strong tourist attraction in the winter months and a magnet for motorcycle riders. Where are all the people? They are actually down the street in the distance feeding the donkeys! Do not feed the baby donkeys solid food as they choke to death. They really do! Never feed any donkey fruit as it makes them ill.

Fig. 47 / Downtown Oatman, Arizona

56. On the south side of downtown you will see a gold mine museum. This is where Lazarus was raised from the dead. Read John 11:38. See Fig. 48. Jesus stood in the street and called for him to arise and he did! Some say the old mine holes in the mountain to the left of this site is the actual resurrection of Lazarus site. What do you believe?

Fig. 48 / Lazarus Tomb

57. In front of the Oatman Hotel is where the donkey talked to Balaam. Read Numbers 22:21. If you place your ear near a donkey's lips you can sometimes hear them whisper words of wisdom. However, do not permit the donkey to nibble on your ear and never stand behind a donkey (just in case it kicks). Did you know that petting a donkey can make you happy? Try it and see! But beware they are wild animals.

Fig. 48-A / A Talking Donkey (aka a smart ass)

58. There may be a wild, wild, west gunfight show in town. If so, check it out.

Fig. 48-B / Wild Donkeys - Highway Robbers

CHAPTER 4

BEGIN TOUR #4

Tour #4

Rest and relax in Oatman to shop and hang around with the donkeys. Remember not to feed them ice cream, fruit or other items. These guys really do best grazing on grass. Signs are posted what you can feed them. When you are ready, we can go on with the Oatman Holy Land Tour or you can come back another time to see the rest. For those who can only stay a little while try to at least take tour #1, #2 and #3.

60. **Reset your odometer to zero in front of the Oatman Hotel.**

61. Head south out of town on the paved road you came in on, historic Route 66. You will come to a fork in the road at 2.4 Miles. You will go left (heading south) following Route 66 for 4.2 miles. You will pass the Lord's Mountain (Boundary Cone Mountain). When you get 4.2 miles (or 6.6 miles from Oatman) turn left to turn around in this parking area.

62. **We will now reset the odometer again to zero** and backtrack (heading north) on Route 66.

63. At 0.2 miles the mountains and a huge landscape is a jumble of ruins. This is all that remains of Sodom and Gomorrah. See Fig. 49. Read Genesis 19:1. Walk around here and you can see black, burnt volcanic boulders (with sulphur brimstone) that have been thrown down to earth.

Fig. 49 / Sodom & Gomorrah - Desolated Land

God was so angry he stoned Sodom and Gomorrah to death using brimstone firebombs. The boulders have holes in them due to escaping volcanic gases. These lava rocks were red-hot and in a plastic state and did fly in the air landing down hard. Notice the oblong and smooth rounded texture and shape. The air sculpted them in mid-air. Like today, nothing is left of old Sodom & Gomorrah. The Lord's anger still smolders and if you read Revelations you will get an idea of His wrath yet to come.

64. Go 0.5 miles and stop. There will be a small hill blocking your view to the east. At the top of this hill is where God made an almond tree rod instantly bloom and bear almonds. Read Numbers 17:8. Walk about this hill and the cactus, but wear leather boots or be very careful if you are wearing shoes, as the cacti needles are everywhere.

65. As viewed from the top of this small hill, in the background, looking east, you can see a narrow but tall volcanic rock peeking out. This is Moses looking at the threshold of the Promised Land, but he is not allowed to enter. See Fig. 50. Read Deuteronomy 3:27 and 34:4.

- If you can't climb the hill, then walk north along the side of the road 50 paces for a good view.

Fig. 50 / Moses

66. Go 0.1 mile to see the Bethlehem cave where Jesus was born. See Fig. 51 and Read Luke 2:8. Angels also visited shepherds here. Read Luke 2:8.

Fig. 51 / Bethlehem Manger

67. At 0.3 miles is a nice scenic view. It is here Jesus fed about 5,000 people, twice. See Fig. 52 and Read Luke 9:13.

Fig. 52 / Jesus Fed 5,000 People

Could you now be standing on the Sermon on the Mount? It appears to be so.

GOOD TREES BEAR GOOD FRUIT

This is also a good place for the church to gather for picnics and outdoor Bible study. Remember also to teach on "doing" the Gospel, not just learning it. Teach others to bear good fruit and to find ways to proclaim the Gospel every day. Start with Gospel tracts and leave them here and there each and every day. That will begin the process and it requires no skill or talent! Read Matthew 25:14. Read the four pages of the Epistle of James in the Bible.

THE SABBATH DAY

Jesus performed some of his greatest healing miracles on the Sabbath. The Sabbath is not Sunday it is from Friday's sunset to Saturday's sunset. Jesus and the Apostles never changed the Sabbath day to Sunday. They observed the Sabbath starting Friday at sunset. You can also make the Sabbath day to be a day of happiness by doing deeds of mercy to others, just as Jesus did. This is a day to enjoy!

68. Go 0.5 miles and you can see the V-notch at the top of the mountain. This is where Elijah was taken up to heaven (rapture). See Fig. 53 and Read II Kings 2:11.

Fig. 53 / Elijah Mountain

69. At 0.3 miles and park. Look up and to your right to the tall mountain. This is the Lion of Tribe of Judah. It is actually the back (south side) of the Lord's mountain. See Fig. 54 revealing this south side view. Now look at Fig. 3 that is the north side and you can compare the two lions. This one mountain actually changes into three shapes, the Lord in a sitting posture (Fig. 1) and two lions (Fig. 3 and 54).

Fig. 54 / Lion of the Tribe of Judah

70. Not shown in Fig. 54, but the lion has a tail of a rock wall that extends for quite a distance and right across Rt. 66. You can see this tail where the angel is on guard in Tour #3 at stop #71, or see Fig. 58.

PROSPERITY GOSPEL

Beware of those who preach nothing else but prosperity quoting the Bible as proof of what they say is correct. Yes, the Lord can create prosperity and He has done so, but if you read the Bible those who received such favor were dedicated servants of the Lord and did not beg for money donations from other believers. They obeyed the Lord's commands faithfully and the Lord God prospered them.

YOU ARE ENTERING THE THRONE ROOM

THE THRONE ROOM OF GOD

70. At 0.3 miles park. The tall mountain to the east is the Throne of God. Fig. 55. Notice the rocks here are the color purple. It is one of the Lord's favorite colors as mentioned in Exodus 25:4, etc.

Fig. 55 / Throne Room of God

- Climb up about 100 paces (it is a bit slippery, but a gentle slope to climb). You will be surrounded with rock formations in the Throne Room. Here these rocks will bear witness to what you say and to what you promise so be careful of what you say to God. Read Joshua 24:7. It will be forever binding upon you!

- This is the place you do not ask God for anything, but here you conform to what God wants you to do for Him. Read Proverbs 11:30, Luke 11:23 and Matthew 20:19. Read Isaiah 1:18. *Come let us reason together!*

- You may want to make a commitment to help the poor and homeless, visit sick and injured people, start a food bank or perform other good deeds the Bible speaks about. The merciful shall obtain mercy.

- If you have a need for God to answer you then go to the Lord's Mountain. We will visit this mountain in a few minutes.

- Fig 56 is an example of a personal promise or a prayer. The stone is used as a paperweight so the wind will not blow it away. Read Malachi 3:10. Spend money to proclaim the Gospel to the lost. Start a gift ministry where you give people gifts that has the Word of God on them. Place the note near a small Creosote bush could even represent the "burning bush" Moses saw. Read Exodus 3:1.

Fig. 56 / Promise to God

- God is now calling "you" into His service to save the lost, visit prisoners, heal the sick, share the Gospel, etc. You do not have to ask God's will for this, He already said to go proclaim the Gospel, so just go do it. Whatever God says in His Word that is "commanded" unto us to do we must do.
- Proclaiming the Gospel to the lost is mandatory duty for all Christians. If you do not gather you scatter. Are you one of those who call the Lord, Lord, yet do not what he says to do? To begin is to begin. Start proclaiming the Gospel to others and "your" personal ministry will grow and bear fruit. Share the Gospel! This is God's will for your life.

....

GIFTS SHOULD ALWAYS HAVE THE WORD OF GOD PRINTED ON THE GIFT SO GOD'S WORD CAN BE SHARED WITH OTHERS

GOSPEL GIFT IDEAS	VISIT A CHRISTIAN BOOK STORE
Weatherproof bookmark.	Money clip.
Gospel verse card.	Vehicle emblem.
Coffee cup.	Air freshener.
Gospel coin.	Vehicle window decal.
Christian book.	Refrigerator magnet.
Christian movie (DVD)	Stationery.
Bumper sticker	Key chain.
License plate frame.	T-shirt.
Bible	Gospel window decal
Gospel tract	Create your own gift.

....

- Fig. 56-A is an example of a Chick.com gospel tract on a creosote bush. People here routinely decorate creosote bushes with Christmas ornaments year 'round. So it is not an unusual practice in the Oatman area. See Fig. 56-B. The spirit of Christmas is strong here all year 'round as demonstrated by the local residents decorating Creosote bushes on Route 66.

Fig. 56-A / Tract on Creosote Bush

Fig. 56-B / Christmas Tree

The Rock of Ages is in the background of the Christmas Tree

- Your company or organization should take advantage to decorate a Creosote tree and place your nameplate by the tree. This will also enhance tourism to come see the decorations and give you subtle advertising exposure. The ornaments, at least at this writing, stay up all year long. This decorating is a local tradition in Oatman.

71. Go 0.3 miles and stop. Here you will see the walls of Jericho See Fig. 57 and Note the cave above in the wall. An invisible angel guards this cave and he will not answer you. If you climb up to the cave to visit the angel you will soon feel uncomfortable and you will be compelled to leave. It is best to observe from a distance. Read Joshua 5:13 to find out whom this angel is!

Fig. 57 / Angel on Guard

Notice the very strange shape of the cave opening.

72. Fig. 58 is a wider view of the Wall of Jericho. When you look from the south on Route 66 at the Lion of the Tribe of Judah in Fig. 54 this rock wall is also the tail of the lion.

Fig. 58 / Wall of Jericho / Tail of the Lion

73. Go 0.4 miles to the Lord's Mountain and park. Here you can leave a gift to the Lord. Here you will leave a gift and pick one up from someone else, a gift exchange ministry. Gifts should have some value and must have the Word of the Lord on it.

Fig. 59 / Leaving Gifts

- Fig. 59 s an example of leaving a gold-plated bookmark gift and two Gospel tracts being left at the Lord's Mountain.
- Did you know that nobody is to come to the Lord without a gift? Read Exodus 34:20, *"And none shall appear before me empty"* means none to appear before God empty-handed, without a gift.
- Don't worry about thieves because they are the lost ones who need the gospel anyway. You can place your gift under a rock if you wish to delay it being easily found.
- If you want to leave a gift elsewhere that is fine too. But do not appear without a gift or appear now and fail to leave a gift later. Keep your promises! Do what the Lord says to do!
- Remember, this is the deal God makes and he makes the rules. You are to deliver to him a gift. When you do, then you can ask of the Lord to help you in your need.

74. Go 1.1 miles and look right and you will again see the Valley of the Shadow of Death. See Fig. 7 and Read Psalm 23:4. It is dark and has many shadows and is not for those with weak faith to venture alone. You can see this valley again just a few tenths of a mile down the road on the right.

PRAYER REQUEST GRANTED

If your prayer has been granted as you requested don't forget to come back to the Lord and give Him thanks. Jesus healed ten lepers and yet only one came back to thank Him. Read Luke 17:12. And don't forget to share the Gospel with others whom also need God's help! Tell others what God has done for you!

You can leave a personal "thank you" note under a stone here, or anywhere, even in your own yard at home. See Fig. 56 as an example. Sometimes you have to be persistent and thank God even when you see no results yet, using your faith that God will deliver you from your trouble.

Tour #4

END OF THE TOUR

Thank you for visiting the Oatman Arizona Holy Land Tour. Please tell all your friends to come visit Oatman Arizona and take the Holy Land Tour!

TO LEARN MORE

If you would like to read more about God and distribute Gospel tracts contact these firms. They will send you a catalog listing tracts and books. Also visit a Christian bookstore for books and gifts you may want to use in your own personal ministry.

- Chick Publications, P.O. Box 3500, Ontario, CA 91761.
- Osterhus Publishing House, 4500 W. Broadway, Minneapolis, MN 55422.
- Moments With The Book, P.O. Box 322, Bedford, PA 15522.
- Sowers of Seed, P.O. Box 6217, Ft. Worth, TX 76115.
- Good News Publishers, 1300 Crescent St. STE B, Wheaton, IL 60187.
- American Tract Society, P.O. Box 462008, Garland, TX 75046.
- People of the Living God / Testimony of Truth Magazine 366 Cove Creek Road, McMinnville, TN 37110.
- Fundamental Evangelistic Assoc., PO Box 6278, Los Osos, CA 93412.
- Proclaiming the Gospel, P.O. Box 940871, Plano, TX 75094.
- If any of the above have relocated you can find them on the Web.
- We have many Christian links on our Web site.

....

FREE SELF-GUIDED TOURS

Yes, we do have free tour guide maps you may print and copy from our Website to share with your friends. If you own a business you can use them for free advertising! Visit James RussellPublishing.com. Then click on Free Tours!

EXTRA OATMAN PAGES

A self-guided auto tour of Route 66 in Oatman, AZ revealing about 60 unusual rock formations that has a Biblical theme to them. Very unusual and entertaining! Go to JamesRussellPublishing.com to read more about the book and to obtain a free sample tour map.

Extra Pages

Fig. 60 / Shall We Meet Again?

Fig. 61 / Bless You People for Loving Us!

Fig. 62 / Oatman, Arizona Opals

Opals in Fig. 62 were found near, but not on the opal mining claim. You can find opals in many areas in these mountains.

Fig. 63 / Prayer Stones - Stack Three Stones When You Pray

Extra Pages

PERSONAL NOTES PAGE

The End Is A New Beginning – James Russell

PERSONAL NOTES PAGE

The End Is A New Beginning – James Russell

BOOK CATALOG

What follows is a few pages of our book catalog. We have many books on our Web site. We do have more historical tour guidebooks for car and motorcycles and more free tour maps, free gifts, free helpful articles on many subjects Check us out!

FREE GIFTS ON OUR WEB SITE

We have free gifts for you on our Web site. Just type into any Internet search engine the words "James Russell Publishing" to find us. Most of our free gifts will be on our Christian Web site, so look for that link when you visit our main home page. JamesRussellPublishing.com

http://www.JamesRussellPublishing.com

Internet Address Book

The Book Every Computer Needs!

PROFESSIONAL VERSION!

If you have a computer you need this book. The Internet Address Book is two books in one. A book to maintain Internet contacts and a log book for recording critical CMOS & BIOS computer files and software specifications.

No address book can match the data saving convienience to the computer user like the Internet Address Book can. Once a computer owner uses this book they will not compute without it!

Put this book on your computer bookshelf and see how fast it sells. The book is exactly what every Internet surfer needs... a handy book to record Web site data.

Read what this book can do...

Cover Price 19.95. ISBN 0-916367-12-6.
118pp., 8x11 format.

You can wait until your computer fails and lose your Internet and computer data or you can save yourself a ton of grief and buy this book now! **James Russell - Author**

* * * *

This book is available in paperback and as an e-book. You will not be disappointed!

SHIPPING NOW!

ORDER TODAY!

THE MARKET IS HUGE

Telephone address books can be found everywhere, but now comes the Internet Address Book!

Just about everyone who owns a computer surfs the Internet and most all suffer from forgetting passwords, software and hardware failure, losing CD-Key numbers, e-mail addresses, you name it. This is the book to solve these problems.

There are no Internet Address Books 100% dedicated to the general Website surfer and the professional business-person... until now!

FEATURES

- Log Internet Website addresses.
- Record computer data to prevent data loss.
- Never forget another password or ID number to enter any Website.
- Record Internet contact and e-mail addresses and even manage sites linking to your Website.
- Safegard Internet data even if your computer is stolen.
- Log your software preferences and CD-Key numbers.
- Recover from virus attacking CMOS or BIOS configurations.
- Supports up to six computers.
- Supports 50 Websites.
- Suports 30 software programs.
- Reover from Internet data loss.

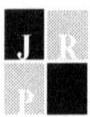

PUBLISHER DISCOUNTS
Bookstore Spec. Order 20%
Individuals $19.95
S & H $4 single copy.

PUBLISHER – SAN 295-852X
James Russell Publishing
wwwJamesRussellPublishing.com

DISTRIBUTORS
Baker & Taylor (800)775-1100
www.btol.com
Ingrams (800)937-8000
www.ingram.com

Trap Shooting Secrets

Endorsed by Professional Shooters

THE FIRST TRAP SHOOTING TECHNICAL BOOK!

There has never been a book like this, ever! *TSS* is like having a shooting coach telling you precisely what to do to hit the targets. In fact, the book is so effective, it is the <u>only</u> book ever to be endorsed by professional trapshooters <u>who make a living</u> in the shooting sports and their testimonials are on the back cover!

Books have been published on trap shooting, but not one has ever been written as a true technical textbook giving detailed step-by-step instructions to shoot high scores. This book turns mediocre shooters into winning champions! The author has performed numerous interviews with the pros to discover the inner secrets and winning ways of the game and has successfully communicated this intangible subject into a powerful book that gives readers results!

Cover Price 34.95. ISBN 0-916367-09-6. 183pp., 8x11 format, over 85 technical illustrations.

I strongly recommend shotgun competition shooters read both Trap Shooting Secrets and Precision Shooting - The Trapshooter's Bible **Luca Scribani Rossi** *– Olympic Medallist & Team Coach.*

* * * *

The concepts in these two books are strongly presented and easily applied. Valuable advice! **Daro Handy – Hall of Fame Professional Trap Shooter**

SHIPPING NOW!

ORDER TODAY!

THE MARKET IS HUGE

Trap shooting is a hidden sport. In the USA there are over 150, 000 extremely dedicated registered trapshooters who compete for money and prizes. Triple that figure for the world.

Wing shooters discovered the book invaluable to hitting targets and they number at **8.5 million**! This book, with it's follow-on companion book, *Precision Shooting - The Trapshooters Bible* are <u>very fast movers</u> in bookstores, often sold the first day displayed on the shelf! Visit our Website to read superb customer testimonials! Order today.

You Won't Be Disappointed!

FEATURES

- Powerful clay target shooting instructions. Secrets of the pros.

- All phases of shooting covered; equipment, concentration, form technique and valuable tips.

- Over 85 illustrations reveals the inner *secrets* of the game.

- Small talk eliminated. The book gets right to the facts and goes deep fast and stays there!

- Professionals have never endorsed any target shooting books prior to this book! That's over 150 years! Endorsed by shooting magazines!

- Readers are given strong instructions, accurate advice and over 135 practice tips they can use immediately! Even videotapes can't match the power and effectiveness of this book! A best-seller!

PUBLISHER DISCOUNTS
Bookstore Spec. Order 20%
Individuals $34.95
S & H $4 single copy.

PUBLISHER – SAN 295-852X
James Russell Publishing
www.JamesRussellPublishing.com

DISTRIBUTORS
Baker & Taylor (800)775-1100
www.btol.com
Ingrams (800)937-8000
www.ingram.com

Precision Shooting - The Trapshooter's Bible

For Professional Shooters

...AND THOSE WHO WANT TO BE!

This is the follow-on book of *Trap Shooting Secrets* and it's **Better Than Ever**!

... Now the *only* trap shooting book with ATA and Olympic-style Double-Trap technical instructions with illustrations!

...The *only* professional advanced-level trap shooting book in the world!

...Proven winning how-to advice for shotgun competition shooters!

...The *only* clay target shooting book with hundreds of answers to technical shooting questions answered in great detail!

...Endorsed by *professional* shotgun shooting instructors!

...Readers obtain high-score *results* with *Precision Shooting*!

Cover Price 34.95. ISBN 0-916367-10X.
220pp., 8x11 format, over 145 technical illustrations, plus 315 questions & answers!

I strongly recommend shotgun competition shooters read both Trap Shooting Secrets and Precision Shooting - The Trapshooter's Bible **Luca Scribani Rossi – Olympic Medallist & Team Coach**

* * * *

The concepts in these two books are strongly presented and easily applied. Valuable advice! **Daro Handy – Hall of Fame Professional Trap Shooter**

SHIPPING NOW!
ORDER TODAY!

THE ULTIMATE

Presicion Shooting and *Trap Shooting Secrets* are endorsed by highly acclaimed qualified pro shooters, instructors and shooting magazines!

No other shotgun shooting books compare with these two books. Why? Because these are the <u>only</u> technical textbooks ever written for the sport and they deliver on the promise!

These books don't talk about shooting, they are comprehensive show-me-how-to-shoot instructional books, like have a shooting coach by your side showing you what to do!

The shotgun books you have on your shelves pale in comparison in regards to effectiveness and fast sales!

Visit our Website to read superb customer testimonials! Order today.

You Won't Be Disappointed!

FEATURES

• Reveals the secrets professionals use to hit targets with consistent accuracy!

• All phases of shooting covered; equipment, concentration, form technique and valuable tips.

• Over 145 illustrations reveals the inner *secrets* of the game.

• More than 315 answers to tough target shooting questions!

• This is no small book. 220 pp in large 8X11 format jammed with shotgun shooting instructions!

• Readers are stunned to discover the secrets of clay target shootisng revealed. Professionals witheld these secrets to maintain their winning edge, but now all is shed to light! Wing shooters love this book!

• #1 best-seller in the sport!

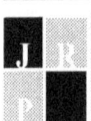

PUBLISHER DISCOUNTS
Bookstore Spec. Order 20%
Individuals $34.95
S & H $4 single copy.

PUBLISHER – SAN 295-852X
James Russell Publishing
www.JamesRussellPublishing.com

DISTRIBUTORS
Baker & Taylor Phone: (800)775-1100
www.btol.com
Ingrams (800)937-8000
www.ingram.com

Steam & Diesel Power Plant Operators Exams

1,400 TEST QUESTIONS & ANSWERS!

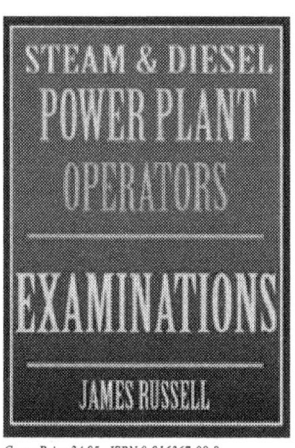

Cover Price 34.95. ISBN 0-916367-08-8. 117pp., 8x11 format, over 1,400 questions & answers.

There are numerous power plants in every city in the world and employees must learn how to operate the machinery. This is the book giving the correct answers to operate a power plant safely.

Stationary engineer boiler operators must pass pre-employment exams, and in some locations licensing exams. This is a powerful book giving readers the results they need... to get hired!

Other steam plant operations books can't measure up to the sheer volume of critical questions & answers in this book. However, this book goes beyond other technical books giving readers "explanations" as to why the answer to the question is correct. This book has been a bestseller to the power plant industry since 1981.

EXAMPLE

Boiler Water Total Dissolved Solids are High. You Should...
A. Increase Sulfite Chemical.
B. Increase steam drum surface blow.
C. Add Sulfite chemical to deareator.
D. Decrease surface blow & perform - A.
E. Answers A & C is to be implemented.
F. Add calcium chloride to boilder water.

Correct Answer is "B".

SHIPPING NOW!

ORDER TODAY!

A STRONG MARKET

Power plants are everywhere. You can use this book to score high on power plant exams!

Civil Service exams must be taken for those entering the stationary engineering field. This book has the answers to score high!

Oil refineries, food processing, electronic firms, metal fabrication mills, electric generating stations and hospitals, military bases all need this book for employee training!

Order today.
You won't be disappointed!

FEATURES

1. 1,400 questions & answers in multiple choice format.

2. You will learn the proper operational procedures and know why they are performed to enhance the safety of yourself and your fellow employees.

A. Many subjects are covered: Steam turbines, boilers, feed pumps, deareators, superheaters, steam engines, cooling tower, refrigeration, cutting in boilers and taking them off the line and much more!

B. Basic stationary emergency electrical generator diesel engines for ship-to-shore power and emergency power for hospitals are included.

C. Even steam engines are covered!

D. Every subject about power plant operations is covered from starting and shutting down boilers and equipment... safely!

PUBLISHER DISCOUNTS
Bookstore Spec. Order 20%
Individuals $34.95
S & H $4 single copy.

PUBLISHER – SAN 295-852X
James Russell Publishing
www.JamesRussellPublishing.com

DISTRIBUTORS
Baker & Taylor (800)775-1100
www.btol.com
Ingrams (800)937-8000
www.ingram.com

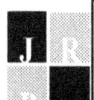

Screen & Stage Marketing Secrets

100% Dedicated To Selling Scripts

THE ONLY SCRIPT MARKETING BOOK!

There are many books on how to write a screenplay, teleplay or stage play script, but only this book tells you how to get your script sold! Step by step instructions are given to perform the marketing process. No theory here, just show-me-how-to-do-it advice!

Writing a script is hard, it's even harder to sell it. *Screen & Stage Marketing Secrets* is an invaluable tool to insure scripts are presented professionally. Rejections will be vastly reduced. All marketing procedures are covered. There are even sample query and cover letters the writer can use. Script marketing is not taught in film schools, now it will be!

More than 200,000 scripts are submitted each year to Hollywood and Broadway and most are rejected due to improper marketing. For decades there has been a dire need for this book. Here it is!

Cover Price 34.95. ISBN 0-916367-11-8. 180pp., 8x11 format, over 40 technical illustrations.

I was surprised to discover just how much I learned. This book is valuable! **Zeolot - Screenwriter**
★ ★ ★ ★
Their should be a book so writers can learn how to submit scripts professionally. This is it! **Literary Agent**
★ ★ ★ ★
Everything you need to know to market your screenplay, TV or stage play script **- James R.**

SHIPPING

NOW!

ORDER TODAY!

THE MARKET

Every major bookstore stocks screenwriting books since most schools offer theater and film courses. That means writers everywhere need this book to get their scripts sold!

This is the *only* technical book 100% dedicated to marketing screenplays, stage plays and television scripts!

Writers will find *Screen & Stage Marketing Secrets* of great value!

Visit our Website to read superb customer testimonials! Order today.

Satisfaction Guaranteed!

FEATURES

- Get an agent or sell your script without one!
- Write powerful and responsive query and cover letters!
- Avoid scriptwriting mistakes!
- Obtain high response from literary agencies!
- Contact production companies without an agent!
- Contact movie stars!
- Get more requests for your scripts!
- Present your scripts professionally to get them sold!
- Access the movie, television and stage play market!
- List of agents willing to give readers of this book *special consideration*! And much more!

PUBLISHER DISCOUNTS
Bookstore Spec. Order 20%
Individuals $34.95
S & H $4 single copy.

PUBLISHER – SAN 295-852X
James Russell Publishing
JamesRussellPublishing.com

DISTRIBUTORS
Baker & Taylor (800)775-1100
www.btol.com
Ingrams (800)937-8000
www.ingram.com

JAMES RUSSELL
PUBLISHING

BOOK CATALOG

Book Catalog

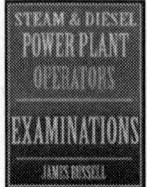

STEAM & DIESEL POWER PLANT OPERATORS EXAMINATIONS
ISBN-10: 0-916367-08-8   ISBN-13: 978-0-916367-08-4
117 pp., 8x11, illustrated, $34.95. Over 1,400 multiple-choice test questions & answers (with explanations) helps stationary engineer power plant operators pass steam boiler licensing and pre-employment exams. This book has the answers to the exams!

TRAP SHOOTING SECRETS
ISBN-10: 0-916367-09-6   ISBN-13: 978-0-916367-09-1
18-3 pp., 8x11, 85 illustrations, $34.95. There has never been a book like this, ever! *TSS* is like having a shooting coach telling you precisely what to do to hit the targets. It is the first book ever to be endorsed by professional trap shooters!

PRECISION SHOOTING - THE TRAPSHOOTER'S BIBLE
ISBN-10: 0-916367-10-X   ISBN-13: 978-0-916367-10-7
230 pp., 8x11, 145 illustrations, $34.95. The *only* trap shooting book with ATA & Olympic Double-Trap technical instructions. The *only* professional advanced-level trapshooting book in the world. Has hundreds of answers to competition shooting questions in great detail to help you understand precisely what professional shooters know.

SCREEN & STAGE MARKETING SECRETS
ISBN-10: 0-916367-11-8   ISBN-13: 978-0-916367-11-4
177 pp., 8x11, 60 illustrations $34.95. The only book specifically written for writers to sell television and feature film movie screenplays and theatrical stage plays to literary agents and production companies. Many books explain how to write scripts, but this one tells how to get them sold! Insider industry secrets of marketing scritps are revealed.

INTERNET ADDRESS BOOK WITH COMPUTER BACK UP FILES
ISBN-10: 0-916367-12-6   ISBN-13: 978-0-916367-12-1
116 pp., 8x11, $19.95 Never lose another important password, ID number, e-mail or Internet contact. Log them here in this book. Also, enter your computer data files so you can recover from computer failure, theft, fire, flood, or just making a file deletion error.

AN EVENING OF COMEDY SKITS – 11 TEN MINUTE THEATRICAL PLAYS
ISBN-10: 0-916367-32-0   ISBN-13: 978-0-916367-32-9
117 pp., 8x11, $34.95. A collection of 11 ten minute comedy sketches. Plays are low budget with common household props and focusing on the funny relationships between men and women. Two parodies included of two TV shows: "Cops" and "The Dating Game". Suitable for general audiences.

James Russell Publishing

STAGE PLAY – A COMEDY THEATRICAL PLAY
ISBN-10: 0-916367-34-7   ISBN-13: 978-0-916367- 34-3
132 pp., 8x11, $12.95 Two women must get married at all cost and they pick two goofy actors using every trick in the book to get the "I do". A fast-pace, low-budget, full-length comedy play focusing on the courtship ritual. No harsh offensive dialog. Common household props. Strong emotional acting.

TRUE BUMS - A COMEDY SCREENPLAY
ISBN-10: 0-916367-26-6   ISBN-13: 978-0-916367-26-8
118 pp., 8x11, $12.95. Three movie executives burned out on life escape the good life of Hollywood to become bobos on a California railroad. Here they discover other rich men doing the same, living the high-life in lavish Disneyland-like fantasy whistle stops, until the wives find out, steal a freight train and the great train chase is on. The bums must save Christmas at all costs from the wives who are determined to capture and return them home, forever!

REVENGE OF THE GRANNIES - A COMEDY SCREENPLAY
ISBN-10: 0-916367-25-8   ISBN-13: 978-0-916367-25-1
124 pp., 8x11, $12.95 Rich grandmothers fed up with crime and a corrupt mayor form a military assault team, MEBOM, to wage full-scale war against the city of Lost Angus street gangs and city hall. Military fireworks and destruction is severe, though nobody is killed in this comedy screenplay. Grandma is the hero!

WALKING WITH THE LORD A CHRISTIAN DEVOTIONAL – DAILY INSPIRATIONAL & WITNESSING INSTRUCTIONS
ISBN-10: 0-916367-19-3   ISBN-13: 978-0-916367-19-0
140 pp., 8x11, $12.95. A powerful daily devotional focusing on what a believer can do for the Lord with hundreds of instructions on how to prepare for God's service. Become a positive and effective witnesses to the Lord. Written for those who believe the Bible to bear good fruit.

HOW TO CHANGE THE OIL IN YOUR TWIN CAM HARLEY DAVIDSON MOTORCYCLE
ISBN-10: 0-916367-75-6   ISBN-13: 978-0-916367-75-6
136 pp., 5.5x8.5, $34.95 A guide on how to change the three oil compartments on the motorcycle. Also replacing the air filter and spark plugs with valuable engine longevity advice. Written for the rider who wants to learn how to do it himself. This book makes it easy to learn with 80 photographs and highly detailed step-by-step instructions.

THE OATMAN ARIZONA HOLY LAND TOUR
ISBN-10: 0-916367-17-7   ISBN-13: 978-0-916367-17-6
104 pp., 5.5x8.5, 60 photographs, $19.95 A Self-guided 60 mile automobile and motorcycle tour of Arizona rock formations resembling Biblical scenes near Oatman, Arizona. A new tourist attraction near Laughlin, Nevada. The tour is on Route 66 and entirely accessible by paved roads. No other tourist attraction in the USA has more Biblical rock formations than in Oatman, Arizona. The tour is on old Route 66.

Book Catalog
BOOK ORDER FORM

QUANTITY   TITLE   RETAIL PRICE
___Steam & Diesel Power Plant Examinations $34.95 _____
___Trap Shooting Secrets $34.95 _____
___Precision Shooting - The Trapshooters Bible $34.95 _____
___Screen & Stage Marketing Secrets $34.95 _____
___Internet Address Book $12.95 _____
___An Evening of Comedy Skits $34.95 _____
___Walking With The Lord Christian Devotional $12.95 _____
___True Bums $12.95 _____
___Revenge of the Grannies $12.95 _____
___Stage Play $12.95 _____
___How to Change the Oil in Your Twin Cam Motorcycle - Harley Davidson $34.95
___The Oatman Arizona Holy Land Tour $19.95

Shipping: $4 per book. $7 for two books. _____
Nevada business: Sales/Use Tax resale number # _____
TOTAL: Shipping Charge and Purchase Price of Books $ _____
Send order and payment to the mailing address listed on our Website.

BOOK TRADE SPECIAL ORDERS

PLEASE SEND A PURCHASE ORDER WITH YOUR SHIPPING ADDRESS, BILLING ADDRESS AND PURCHASE ORDER NUMBER.

TRADE DISCOUNT:
Bookstores 20% "Special Order" discount. Net/30
Wholesalers 37%. Terms Net/90

PLEASE PURCHASE OUR BOOKS FROM OUR WHOLESALERS:
For Print on Demand books contact Lightning Source listed here.
Baker & Taylor: www.btol.com Phone 908-218-3950
Ingram: www.ingrambookgroup.com Phone 800-937-8000
Lightning Source USA www.lightningsource.com Phone 615-213-5815
Lightning Source UK www.lightningsource.co.uk Phone +44(0)1908 443555
Brodart Company: www.brodart.com Phone 800-233-8467
Spring Arbor wholesales our *Walking With The Lord* book. Phone 800-395-4340

James Russell, 205 Rainbow Drive, # 10585, Livingston, TX 77399
SAN 295-852X. Web site: JamesRussellPublishing.com

www.ingramcontent.com/pod-product-compliance
Lightning Source LLC
Chambersburg PA
CBHW032057150426
43194CB00006B/554